A Gift

For: Linda

From: Lori & Bob

OTHER BOOKS BY BRADLEY TREVOR GREIVE

The Blue Day Book
The Blue Day Journal and Directory
Dear Mom
Looking for Mr. Right
The Meaning of Life

The Incredible Truth About
Motherhood

BRADLEY TREVOR GREIVE

BOK4092

Andrews McMeel
Publishing

THE INCREDIBLE TRUTH ABOUT MOTHERHOOD

This edition published in 2003 by Andrews McMeel Publishing exclusively for Hallmark Cards, Inc.

www.hallmark.com

ISBN: 0-7407-3791-0

Book design by Holly Camerlinck

PHOTO CREDITS

GETTYONE (Sydney, www.gettyimages.com): pages 3, 11, 13, 18, 27, 30, 32, 34, 35, 38, 43, 44, 48, 54, 55, 59, 61, 64, 68, 69, 72, 73, 89, 91, 92, 93, 99.

PHOTOLIBRARY.COM (Sydney, www.photolibrary.com): Cover, pages 16, 40, 57, 62, 80, 81, 82, 87, 88, 90, 106.

WILDLIGHT PHOTO AGENCY (Sydney, www.wildlight.net): pages 19, 24, 49, 63, 71, 77, 84, 85, 97.

IMAGE BANK (Sydney, www.gettyimages.com): pages 2, 7, 12, 17, 21, 22, 31, 33, 41, 45, 46, 47, 50, 51, 65, 74, 75, 95, 104.

STOCK PHOTOS PHOTOGRAPHIC LIBRARY (Sydney, www.stockphotos.com.au): pages 4, 5, 6, 8, 15, 52, 70, 83, 100, 101, 105.

AUSTRAL INTERNATIONAL (Sydney, www.australphoto.com): pages 9, 28, 60, 98.

AUSTRALIAN PICTURE LIBRARY (Sydney, www.australianpicturelibrary.com.au): pages 25, 29, 36, 37, 39, 42, 53, 56, 58, 66, 76, 78, 79, 94, 96, 102, 103, 107.

SMH FAIRFAX (Sydney, www.smh.com.au): pages 20, 23.

AUSCAPE (Sydney, www.auscape.com.au): page 14.

WEST AUSTRALIAN NEWS (Perth, www.thewest.com.au): pages 10, 86.

BASQUALI Pty. Ltd. (Sydney, www.basquali.com): page 68.

STONE (Sydney, www.gettyimages.com): page 26.

The hand that rocks the cradle
is the hand that rules the world.

—WILLIAM ROSS WALLACE

A child's dreams are tomorrow's reality.

Children are the future. Our future.
By which I mean our future champions,

supermodels,

Elvis impersonators,

IRS agents, and so on.

So in no small way, our world is in their tiny hands.
But whose hands are they in?

8   The answer, of course, is someone with extreme patience,

gentle understanding,

and never-ending love. Namely, their mothers.

This epic relationship begins with childbirth,
an experience most mothers describe as exhilarating, 11

exhausting,

more painful than a lap-full of hot coffee,

and yet so special and so rewarding
that it cannot easily be described in words.

Yes indeed, the opportunity to guide this new life toward
its destiny can only be seen as a precious gift from God.

At that moment, the intense feelings of love
and purpose can make it impossible for mothers
to contain their heartfelt joy,

which is why the first ear-splitting cries at three A.M.
can be a wake-up call in more ways than one.

Breast-feeding isn't exactly a walk in the park, either.

And let me tell you, nothing makes the
magic of motherhood disappear faster than
changing your first stinky-poo diaper.

19

Yuck! Yuck!! Yuck!!!

Now, once a woman has children she can't run,

and she can't hide.

They will be in the picture for virtually every hour
of every day for at least the next two decades.

That means no long hot soaks in the bath,

no unobstructed TV viewing, 25

and absolutely no chance of an intimate moment
going uninterrupted.

In fact, from that moment on she can barely put her feet up for a second without hearing distant cries for attention or the expensive tinkle of a priceless crystal heirloom being smashed to smithereens by a rampaging toddler.

Oh yes, the joyful pitter-patter of tiny feet
starts to sound a little more ominous.

And so, for the new mother,
Mondays are incredibly tiring.

Tuesdays, Wednesdays, Thursdays, and Fridays
are even worse. And the weekends?

"Don't even ask!" 31

Every morning a mother wakes up to a new battle.

There's basically no end to the dangerous,

unbelievably bizarre situations that kids can get into.

At times it seems as if a mother's vocabulary is
limited to "Oh my Gawd!"

And "Get down from there this instant!"

Thus, in order to save her children from themselves, she will perform a dozen high-speed rescues every single day. (Makes the Coast Guard seem kind of lazy, doesn't it?)

THE SHOPPING PRAYER
"Dear Lord, please help me get through the shopping
quickly today without another embarrassing disaster like
last week's in the frozen foods section. Amen."

Shopping with children involves three things:
First, being dragged into toy stores again and again. 39

Second, it means kids running madly through stores

knocking over displays and generally creating havoc,

which provides the perfect cover for at least one child
to wander off into the mall and get hopelessly lost.

And last but not least, it means,
"Mommy, can I have an ice cream, puh-lease?!"

"I want an ice cream!"

"Ice cream! Ice cream! Ice cream! Ice cream! Ice cream! Ice cream! Ice cream! Ice cream! Ice cream! Ice cream! Ice cream! Ice cream! . . ."

Ooooh, baby. Talk about a headache for life!
(And people wonder why Prozac sales are booming.)

Now, while all this is going on, you might be wondering what it is that fathers actually do. Are they just sitting around all day twiddling their opposable thumbs? No, sir!

They also grunt and say, "Go ask your mother."

And sometimes they shout, "Damn it, Honey! Can't you keep these kids quiet? I'm trying to watch the game here!"

Okee-dokee, so now you know. Hmmm.
Anyway, let's get back to Mom and the joys of mealtime.

"Children dear, come inside
and get ready for dinner, please!"

48 MINUTES LATER
"For the last time, get your butts in here
and eat, damn it!"

"Don't give me any broccoli!"

"Are we having french fries? I want french fries!"

"Awww, not pot roast again. I hate pot roast. Blecch!"

Family dining does not always provide the
"positive communication opportunities" described by
TV talk-show hosts.

Amazingly, a mother can prepare over twenty thousand family meals before her kids leave home, and still there would be children (and husbands) who think that dinner just magically appears on the table every night!

To them, it's as if you could just snap your fingers
and a roast chicken would fall out of the sky.

After dinner is over, getting the kids bathed and
ready for bed requires a firm hand, to say the least.

But eventually the precious little ones fall fast asleep,
as innocent and beautiful as baby angels.

Whew! Finally Mom has a chance to inhale some sanity
and maybe even enjoy a few romantic moments with
the man of the house under the covers . . .

or maybe not.

In which case, she will collapse into a
deep healing sleep . . .

before being awakened in the middle of the night by a screaming child having a nightmare about being chased by an evil monster from their Harry Potter book, which they describe as looking somewhat like their school principal but with bigger teeth.

That's when Mom discovers that she also has to
counsel them through the shame of bed-wetting.

You know, leading social scientists estimate that one day
like this is equal to six months in a Russian salt mine.
Little wonder that some mothers turn gray overnight.

Especially considering that, as we all know, 999 out of every 1,000 children born have the potential to be rotten little monsters,

and one will be abducted by aliens.

Certainly, as children mature into teenagers
they can become very sneaky indeed.

Little white lies about washing behind ears
and brushing teeth

become absolute whoppers as young adults test and
retest the boundaries of their mothers' gullibility.

"Ooooh, Mama (cough, cough), I feel so sick. Boy, am I sick (cough, cough). I reckon I'm much too sick to go and take my geography test (cough, cough), and I studied so hard for it, too (cough, cough)."

Of course, sometimes kids really are sick
and that's no fun for Mom, either.

Grooming a child for adulthood is not easy,
and whether it's wild hairstyles,

funky piercings,

or catching them trying to sneak back into the house
after a secret date,

75

this period is perhaps the most worrying for a mother.

What if her child grows up to be an inept criminal mastermind?

A White House spokesperson?

Or, God forbid, become a regular on *Baywatch*?!

To make a mother's job even harder, she has a million
irritating friends and relatives looking over her shoulder
all the time, ready to give advice on the best way
to raise kids today.

"Look, honey, you gotta spank naughty kids. Forget what the books say, you gotta spank 'em real good or they'll turn out rotten! Why, I got spanked with a shoe every day of my life until I was twenty-one and I'm damn grateful for it, too!"

If all this sounds rather stressful, that's because it is.
Some moms go completely nuts until their kids
leave for college, and who can blame them?

Frankly, when you consider their burden, it's surprising
that more mothers don't develop an eating disorder,

break out in an embarrassing stress-related rash,

develop an unquenchable thirst for tequila,

or at least have an affair with their therapist.

But throughout all of this, a mother never loses
sight of her loving purpose: to walk beside her child
through life's difficult journey,

every step of the way.

Sometimes a child has an obvious talent
and a clear passion to pursue it.

Mostly, it takes a little time to emerge.

Along the way, there will definitely be moments that everyone would rather forget about.

But eventually, after much effort, a mother
will finally be able to see her children find their
place in the world.

Sooner or later, they too will find someone special
to enjoy it with.

Then, and this will break your heart, a mother knows
that she must say good-bye. The child for whom she has
been an endless source of love, wisdom, and inspiration
has now grown up.

As she sits back to watch her child leave, the silence
of her home echoes with memories of little hands,
first words, and wobbly steps on tiny toes.

So how on earth can we possibly begin to thank mothers for bringing children into existence, for raising all intelligent life on this planet, and thus guaranteeing the survival of our species?

Now that makes you stop and think, doesn't it?

Well, let's see. A five-star, all expenses paid,
luxury holiday for the rest of her life would
probably be a good place to start.

Or perhaps some beautiful flowers every now and then
(not just on Mother's Day)

and a big "Thank You" kiss would
make her feel very special.

(But not as big and sloppy as the kisses forced on you
by over-affectionate relatives with fish breath.)

Of course, a far greater reward is for her little bundle of joy to fulfill his or her potential by growing up to be someone she can be proud of:

someone who is honest and loving, someone who
treats others with kindness and respect, someone
who will stand up for what they believe in, 103

someone who, in their own small way,
makes the world a better place.

But all she really wants, all she hopes for, is to know
in her heart that her children are truly happy.

That's it, in a nutshell. I know it sounds incredible, but it's true. In return for all her countless hours of devotion and sacrifice, a mother just wants her children to be happy.

Oh, and to occasionally hear four very special words:

"I love you, Mom!"

ACKNOWLEDGMENTS

It seems that there are many influential people who don't want the "incredible truth" to be known. At times, when I was sick of leaping from moving trains and tired of sleeping in cornfields, I wanted to give up my quest. But thanks to true believers like Jane Palfreyman from Random House (Australia), my heart was fortified, and I was able to complete this epic task. Still, were it not for Christine Schillig (aka "La Mujer de la Fuego") and her "Andrews McMeel All-Stars," who once smuggled me across state lines in the back of their tour bus, this book would never have seen daylight.

The following people also risked their lives by helping me gain access to top-secret photographic archives: Basquali, Andrew Stephenson, Anne Sidlo, Simone Cater, Rachel Badham, Sashi Kanagasabai, David Taylor, Adrian Seaforth, Karl Mellington, Bronwyn Stewart, and Norma Scott. Special thanks are also due to my lethal yet personable assistant, Anita Arnold.

It is fitting that I close with a few remarks about the great Al Zuckerman of Writers House, New York. Al is a selfless literary super-agent by day and a fearless crusader for justice by night. On more than one occasion, I've seen him spit a chili mussel through a plate glass window in the name of freedom. If it weren't for his allergy to spandex he definitely would be bigger than Batman by now. Al, wherever you are, I thank you.